macarons

macarons

Francis van Arkel

NH
NEW
HOLLAND

Published in 2013 by New Holland Publishers
London • Sydney • Auckland • Cape Town
www.newhollandpublishers.com

Garfield House 86–88 Edgware Road London W2 2EA United Kingdom
1/66 Gibbes Street Chatswood NSW 2067 Australia
218 Lake Road Northcote Auckland New Zealand
Wembley Square First Floor Sloan Road Gardens Cape Town 8001 South Africa

First published by Veltman Uitgevers as *Macarons*
www.veltman-uitgevers.nl
Copyright © 2013 New Holland Publishers

ISBN 9781742573984

Text, recipes and food styling: Francis van Arkel and Eric Arts
Styling: Lize Boer
Photography: Bart Nijs Fotografie, Remco Lassche, commissioned by NutriVisie

Translation: Ammerins Moss-de Boer, Leeuwarden
Design: Keisha Galbraith
Publishing Director: Lliane Clarke
Production Director: Olga Dementiev
Printed by Toppan Leefung (China) Ltd

10 9 8 7 6 5 4 3 2
Follow New Holland Publishers on Facebook: www.facebook.com/NewHollandPublishers

For more information:

Made possible with the help of: Restaurant de Roerganger, Roermond, www.deroerganger.nl ,
Dille & Kamille, www.dille-kamille.nl , ZININ, Utrecht, www.zinin-utrecht.nl , V&D, www.vd.nl

contents

foreword

These tasty and hip cookies are originally from France, where people have been enjoying them for decades. At the top macaron shops in Paris, people queue for a long time to buy these sweet delicacies. With the recipes in this book, you'll be able to make them yourself. They have all been tried and tested, so success is guaranteed!

What is a macaron? A macaron is a light and crispy cookie, made with egg white, almond flour and icing sugar. Wheat flour is not used, which means macarons are also gluten-free – depending on the type of filling you use, of course. This filling can be made in various ways. You can vary the taste and colour, but... never break the number one patissier's rule: stick to the proportions of the ingredients and be precise when measuring and weighing them out. The results will be worth it!

Have fun baking!

Francis van Arkel

macarons with fruit

green apple & raisins

makes 30 macarons

For the macarons:
Ingredients for the basic recipe on page 9
a few drops of apple essence

For the filling:
160g/5½oz butter
60g/2oz apple coulis
60g/2oz raisins
a dash of Calvados

Make the macarons with the basic recipe on page 9, but before piping fold in as much essence and food dye as required to get the desired effect.

Plump up the raisins in the Calvados, drain and finely chop.

Make the apple coulis by blending and boiling 60g/2oz of peeled apple. Drain well. Use 60g/2oz of apple coulis per 160g/5½oz of butter cream.

Make the filling by beating the butter until it is soft and creamy. Fold in the apple coulis and raisins.

Pipe the filling onto a macaron and press on a second macaron, allowing the filling to be pushed to the outside edges.

macarons with fruit

roses & lychee

makes 30 macarons

For the macarons:
Ingredients for the basic recipe on page 9
pink food dye paste

For the filling:
160g/5½oz butter
40g/1½oz lychee coulis (see below)
4 teaspoons rose syrup
pink food dye paste

Make the macarons with the basic recipe on page 9, but before piping fold in as much essence and food dye as required to get the desired effect.

Make the filling by beating the butter until it is soft and creamy. Make the lychee coulis by mashing 40g/1½oz of canned lychees and drain well. Fold in the lychee coulis to the creamed butter. Flavour the butter cream with rose syrup and add some pink food dye for added colour. If you are not adding rose syrup, use 60g/2oz of lychee coulis per 160g/5½oz of butter cream.

Pipe the filling onto a macaron and press on a second macaron, allowing the filling to be pushed to the outside edges.

macarons with fruit

pineapple

makes 30 macarons

For the macarons:
Ingredients for the basic recipe on page 9
yellow food dye paste

For the filling:
160g/5½oz butter
60g/2oz pineapple coulis

Make the macarons with the basic recipe on page 9, but before piping fold in as much essence and food dye as required to get the desired effect.

Make the filling by beating the butter until it is soft and creamy. Make the pineapple coulis by mashing 60g/2oz of pineapple (fresh or from a tin). Drain. Use 60g/2oz of pineapple coulis per 160g/5½oz of butter cream. Fold the pineapple coulis into the butter cream.

Pipe the filling onto a macaron and press on a second macaron, allowing the filling to be pushed to the outside edges.

macarons with fruit

banana

makes 30 macarons

For the macarons:
Ingredients for the basic recipe on page 9
a few drops of banana essence
yellow food dye paste

For the filling:
160g/5½oz butter
60g/2oz banana coulis (see below)
lemon juice

Make the macarons with the basic recipe on page 9, but before piping fold in as much essence and food dye as required to get the desired effect.

Make the filling by beating the butter until it is soft and creamy.

Make the banana coulis by mashing 60g/2oz of banana with a dash of lemon juice. Use 60g/2oz of banana coulis per 160g/5½oz of butter cream. Fold the banana coulis into the butter cream.

Pipe the filling onto a macaron and press on a second macaron, allowing the filling to be pushed to the outside edges.

macarons with fruit

tropical fruit

makes 30 macarons

For the macarons:
Ingredients for the basic recipe on page 9
orange food dye paste

For the filling:
160g/5½oz butter
60g/2oz tropical fruit coulis

Make the macarons with the basic recipe on page 9, but before piping fold in as much essence and food dye as required to get the desired effect.

Make the filling by beating the butter until it is soft and creamy. Make the coulis by mashing 60g/2oz of tropical fruit (fresh or from a tin). Drain. Use 60g/2oz of fruit coulis per 160g/5½oz of butter cream. Fold the tropical fruit coulis into the butter cream

Pipe the filling onto a macaron and press on a second macaron, allowing the filling to be pushed to the outside edges.

macarons with fruit

macarons with herbs & spices

lavender & chocolate

makes 30 macarons

For the macarons:

Ingredients for the basic recipe on page 9

40g/1½oz sugar

40g/1½oz water

1/2 tsp crushed

1 tsp dried lavender flowers

violet food dye paste

For the filling:

160g/5½oz butter

1 tbsp cocoa powder, sieved

Bring the sugar, water and lavender flowers to the boil and reduce to a lavender syrup. Sieve the mixture and let the syrup cool down.

Make the macarons with the basic recipe on page 9 and fold in ½ teaspoon of the lavender syrup. Before piping, fold in as much food dye as required to get the desired colour. Sprinkle a few lavender flowers over the piped macarons.

Make the filling by beating the butter until it is soft and creamy. Fold in the cocoa powder. Pipe the filling onto a macaron and press on a second macaron, allowing the filling to be pushed to the outside edges.

macarons with herbs and spices

mint & olive oil

makes 30 macarons

For the macarons:

Ingredients for the basic recipe on page 9

a few drops of mint essence (optional)

green food dye paste

For the filling:

160g/5½oz butter

4 tsp extra virgin olive oil

1 tsp finely chopped mint leaves

Make the macarons with the basic recipe on page 9, but before piping fold in as much essence and food dye as required to get the desired effect.

Make the filling by beating the butter until it is soft and creamy. Stir in the olive oil and chopped mint.

Pipe the filling onto a macaron and press on a second macaron, allowing the filling to be pushed to the outside edges.

spiced cookies

for 30 macaroons

For the macarons:
Ingredients for the basic recipe on page 9
1 tsp mixed spice

For the filling:
160g/5½oz butter
4 crushed Speculoos (Dutch windmill) cookies

Make the macarons with the basic recipe on page 9, but before piping fold in the mixed spice.

Make the filling by beating the butter until it is soft and creamy. Fold in the finely crushed cookies.

Pipe the filling onto a macaron and press on a second macaron, allowing the filling to be pushed to the outside edges.

macarons with herbs and spices

fennel and aniseed

makes 30 macarons

For the macarons:

Ingredients for the basic recipe on page 9

2 tbsp aniseed

For the filling:

160g/5½oz butter

60g/2oz fennel coulis

Make the macarons with the basic recipe on page 9. After piping, sprinkle some aniseed over the macarons.

Make the filling by beating the butter until it is soft and creamy. Make the fennel coulis by braising, mashing and sieving 100g/3½oz of fennel. Use 60g/2oz of fennel coulis per 160g/5½oz of butter cream. Fold the fennel coulis into the butter cream.

Pipe the filling onto a macaron and press on a second macaron, allowing the filling to be pushed to the outside edges.

thyme & honey

makes 30 macarons

For the macarons:

Ingredients for the basic recipe on page 9

2 tbsp finely chopped thyme

For the filling:

160g/5½oz butter

4 tsp runny honey

Make the macarons with the basic recipe on page 9, but before piping fold in the finely chopped thyme.

Make the filling by beating the butter until it is soft and creamy. Stir in the honey.

Pipe the filling onto a macaron and press on a second macaron, allowing the filling to be pushed to the outside edges.

liquorice

makes 30 macarons

For the macarons:

Ingredients for the basic recipe on page 9

1 tbsp liquorice powder

black food dye paste

For the filling:

160g/5½oz butter

4 tsp liquorice syrup

Make the macarons with the basic recipe on page 9, but before piping fold in the liquorice powder and as much food dye as required to get the desired effect.

Make the filling by beating the butter until it is soft and creamy. Stir in the liquorice syrup.

Pipe the filling onto a macaron and press on a second macaron, allowing the filling to be pushed to the outside edges.

macarons with herbs and spices

macarons
with alcohol

sambuca & coffee beans

makes 30 macarons

For the macarons:
Ingredients for the basic recipe on page 9
brown food dye paste

For the filling:
160g/5½oz butter
4 tsp Sambuca
4-6 grated coffee beans
30 chocolate coffee beans

Make the macarons with the basic recipe on page 9, but before piping fold in as much essence and food dye as required to get the desired effect.

Make the filling by beating the butter until it is soft and creamy. Fold in the Sambuca and grated coffee beans.

Pipe the filling onto a macaron and press on a second macaron, allowing the filling to be pushed to the outside edges. Stick a chocolate coffee bean on top of each macaron, using a bit of filling as glue.

macarons with alcohol

amaretto & almond

makes 30 macarons

For the macarons:

Ingredients for the basic recipe on page 9

For the filling:

160g/5½oz butter

20g/²/₃oz shaved almonds, finely chopped

4 tsp Amaretto

Make the macarons with the basic recipe on page 9.

Make the filling by beating the butter until it is soft and creamy. Fold in the shaved almonds and Amaretto.

Pipe the filling onto a macaron and press on a second macaron, allowing the filling to be pushed to the outside edges.

macarons with alcohol

port & figs

makes 30 macarons

For the macarons:
Ingredients for the basic recipe on page 9
dark red food dye paste

For the filling:
160g/5½oz butter
4 fresh figs, cut into pieces
100g/3½oz red port

Make the macarons with the basic recipe on page 9, but before piping fold in as much essence and food dye as required to get the desired effect.

Make the filling by beating the butter until it is soft and creamy. Boil the figs in the red port. Mash up the fig sauce, and use 80g/2½ oz grams per 160g/5½oz of butter cream. Stir through the butter cream.

Pipe the filling onto a macaron and press on a second macaron, allowing the filling to be pushed to the outside edges.

macarons with alcohol

sweet wine & chocolate

makes 30 macarons

For the macarons:
Ingredients for the basic recipe on page 9
brown food dye paste

For the filling:
160g/5½oz butter
200g/7oz sweet dessert wine (we use Banyuls)
4 g cocoa powder

Make the macarons with the basic recipe on page 9, but before piping fold in as much essence and food dye as required to get the desired effect.

Make the filling by beating the butter until it is soft and creamy. Reduce the sweet wine until you have 40g/1½oz left and leave it to cool. Stir the wine and cocoa powder through the butter cream.

Pipe the filling onto a macaron and press on a second macaron, allowing the filling to be pushed to the outside edges.

macarons with alcohol

macarons with chocolate, nuts coffee & tea

banoffee

For the macarons:

Ingredients for the basic recipe on page 9

light brown food dye paste

For the filling:

160g/5½oz butter

30g/1oz banana coulis

30g/1oz caramel sauce (from any good delicatessen)

Make the macarons with the basic recipe on page 9, but before piping fold in as much essence and food dye as required to get the desired effect.

Make the filling by beating the butter until it is soft and creamy. Make the banana coulis by mashing 30g/1oz of banana with a dash of lemon juice. Fold the banana coulis and caramel sauce into the butter cream.

Pipe the filling onto a macaron and press on a second macaron, allowing the filling to be pushed to the outside edges.

macarons with chocolate, nuts, coffee & tea

pistachio

makes 30 macarons

For the macarons:

Ingredients for the basic recipe on page 9

2 tbsp finely chopped pistachios, plus extra for garnish

a few drops of pistachio essence (optional)

For the filling:

160g/5½oz butter

40g/1½oz pistachios, finely chopped

a few drops of pistachio essence (optional)

green food dye paste

Make the macarons with the basic recipe on page 9, but before piping fold in as much essence as required to get the desired taste. Fold in most of the chopped pistachios and sprinkle the rest of the chopped nuts over the piped macarons.

Make the filling by beating the butter until it is soft and creamy. Fold in the pistachios and as much essence and food dye as required to get the desired effect.

Pipe the filling onto a macaron and press on a second macaron, allowing the filling to be pushed to the outside edges. Sprinkle the rest of the pistachios over the macarons.

latte macchiato

makes 30 macarons

For the macarons:

Ingredients for the basic recipe on page 9

1 tbsp instant coffee powder

For the filling:

160g/5½oz butter

60g/2oz condensed milk (can)

Make the macarons with the basic recipe on page 9, but before piping fold in the coffee powder.

Make the filling by beating the butter until it is soft and creamy. Fold in the condensed milk.

Pipe the filling onto a macaron and press on a second macaron, allowing the filling to be pushed to the outside edges.

chocolate hazelnut praline

makes 30 macarons

For the macarons:

Ingredients for the basic recipe on page 9

1 tbsp cocoa powder, sieved

For the filling:

160g/5½oz butter

60g/2oz hazelnut spread

Make the macarons with the basic recipe on page 9, but before piping fold in the cocoa powder.

Make the filling by beating the butter until it is soft and creamy. Fold in the hazelnut spread.

Pipe the filling onto a macaron and press on a second macaron, allowing the filling to be pushed to the outside edges. Sprinkle over a bit of cocoa powder, using a tea strainer.

green tea

For the macarons:
Ingredients for the basic recipe on page 9
green food dye paste

For the filling:
160g/5½oz butter
200ml(7fl oz) green tea
50g/1¾oz white sugar

Make the macarons with the basic recipe on page 9, but before piping fold in as much food dye as required to get the desired colour.

Make the filling by beating the butter until it is soft and creamy. Boil the green tea with the sugar until you have 40g/1½oz left. Let the reduced tea syrup cool down and fold through the butter cream.

Pipe the filling onto a macaron and press on a second macaron, allowing the filling to be pushed to the outside edges.

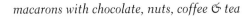

appetizer macarons

tomato & basil

makes about 50 macarons

For the macarons:

90g/3oz water

90g/3oz tomato juice

50g/1¾oz sugar

1 tsp vinegar

40g/1½oz egg white (protein) powder

1 tbsp basil, torn

For the filling:

400g/14oz mascarpone

80g/2½ oz sundried tomatoes, finely chopped

1 tbsp basil, torn

salt and pepper

Mix the water, tomato juice, sugar, vinegar, egg white powder and basil and beat until the mixtures forms peaks. Spoon the mixture into a piping bag with a round nozzle and pipe rounds on the baking paper. Leave the macarons to dry for 2-3 hours (or longer) in an oven set to 80-90°C/175°F. Leave the macarons to cool on the baking paper before peeling them off.

Make the filling by beating the mascarpone and folding in the sundried tomatoes and basil. Season with salt and pepper.

Because these macarons become soft very quickly after adding the filling, serve them straight after filling them! Pipe a swirl of filling on one biscuit and put a second one on top. You can also serve the filling separate in a bowl. This way, the macarons can be eaten as savoury 'toast'.

appetizer macarons

rocket, pine nuts & parmesan

makes about 50 macarons

For the macarons:

180g/6oz water

30g/1oz rocket

50g/1¾oz sugar

1 tsp vinegar

40g/1½oz egg white (protein) powder

2 tbsp roasted pine nuts

For the filling:

400g/14oz mascarpone

20g/²/₃oz roasted pine nuts, chopped

4 tbsp finely chopped rocket

40g/1½oz grated Parmesan cheese

salt and pepper

Mix the water with the rocket in a blender and pass it through a sieve. Use 180g/6oz of the rocket water. Mix the rocket water, sugar, vinegar and egg white powder and beat until the mixture forms peaks. Spoon the mixture into a piping bag with a round nozzle and pipe rounds on the baking paper. Sprinkle over the pine nuts. Leave the macarons to dry complete for 2-3 hours (or longer) in an oven set to 80-90°C/175°F. Leave the macarons to cool on the baking paper before peeling them off.

Make the filling by beating the mascarpone and folding in the pine nuts, rocket and cheese. Season with salt and pepper.

Because these macarons become soft very quickly after adding the filling, serve them straight after filling them! Pipe a swirl of filling on one biscuit and put a second one on top. You can also serve the filling separate in a bowl. This way, the macarons can be eaten as savoury 'toast'.

appetizer macarons

beetroot & foie gras

makes about 50 macarons

For the macarons:

180g/6oz beetroot juice

50g/1¾oz sugar

1 tsp vinegar

40g/1½oz egg white (protein) powder

For the filling:

200g/7oz mascarpone

200g/7oz foie gras (or other type of pâté)

salt and pepper

Mix the beetroot juice, sugar, vinegar and egg white powder and beat until the mixtures forms peaks. Spoon the mixture into a piping bag with a round nozzle and pipe rounds on the baking paper. Leave the macarons to dry complete for 2-3 hours (or longer) in an oven set to 80-90°C/175°F. Leave the macarons to cool on the baking paper before peeling them off.

Make the filling by beating the mascarpone and folding in the pâté. Season with salt and pepper.

Because these macarons become soft very quickly after adding the filling, serve them straight after filling them! Pipe a swirl of filling on one biscuit and put a second one on top. You can also serve the filling separate in a bowl. This way, the macarons can be eaten as savoury 'toast'.

appetizer macarons

saffron & seafood cream

makes about 50 macarons

For the macarons:

180g/6oz water

10 saffron threads

50g/1¾oz sugar

1 tsp vinegar

40g/1½oz egg white (protein) powder

For the filling:

400g/14oz mascarpone

80g/ 2½ oz finely chopped fried scampi/
   shrimp cooled and patted dry

2 tbsp finely chopped dill

salt and pepper

Mix the water (with the saffron), sugar, vinegar and egg white powder and beat until the mixtures forms peaks. Spoon the mixture into a piping bag with a round nozzle and pipe rounds on the baking paper. Leave the macarons to dry complete for 2-3 hours (or longer) in an oven set to 80-90°C/175°F. Leave the macarons to cool on the baking paper before peeling them off.

Make the filling by beating the mascarpone and folding in the scampi/shrimp and dill. Season with salt and pepper.

Because these macarons become soft very quickly after adding the filling, serve them straight after filling them! Pipe a swirl of filling on one biscuit and put a second one on top. You can also serve the filling separate in a bowl. This way, the macarons can be eaten as savoury 'toast'.

lemongrass & coconut cream

makes about 50 macarons

For the macarons:

180g/6oz water

5 stalks of lemon grass, bruised

50g/1¾oz sugar

1 tsp vinegar

40g/1½oz egg white (protein) powder

For the filling:

350g/12oz chicken fillets, cut into pieces

400ml/14fl oz coconut milk (1 can)

1 stalk of lemon grass, bruised

1-2 tbsp red curry paste

Bring the water to the boil and add the lemon grass. Let this soak for 30 minutes. Let the liquid cool down. Mix the lemon grass water (without the stalks of lemon grass), sugar, vinegar and egg white powder and beat until the mixtures forms peaks. Spoon the mixture into a piping bag with a round nozzle and pipe rounds on the baking paper. Leave the macarons to dry complete for 2-3 hours (or longer) in an oven set to 80-90°C/175°F. Leave the macarons to cool on the baking paper before peeling them off.

Make the filling by boiling the chicken in the coconut milk for 15 minutes with the lemon grass. Remove the lemon grass. Put the chicken in a blender with the curry paste and some of the coconut juice and mix. You should get a paste that can be easily piped onto the macarons. Season with salt and pepper.

Because these macarons become soft very quickly after adding the filling, serve them straight after filling them! Pipe a swirl of filling on one biscuit and put a second one on top. You can also serve the filling separate in a bowl. This way, the macarons can be eaten as savoury 'toast'.

appetizer macarons

spicy squid & mussels

makes about 50 macarons

For the macarons:

180g/6oz water

50g/1¾oz sugar

1 tsp vinegar

40g/1½oz egg white (protein) powder

1 full tsp of squid ink

For the filling:

400g/14oz mascarpone

200g/7oz finely chopped cooked mussels

1-2 tsp paprika, cumin spice mix

Mix the water, sugar, vinegar, egg white powder and squid ink and beat until the mixtures forms peaks. Spoon the mixture into a piping bag with a round nozzle and pipe rounds on the baking paper. Leave the macarons to dry complete for 2-3 hours (or longer) in an oven set to 80-90°C/175°F. Leave the macarons to cool on the baking paper before peeling them off.

Make the filling by beating the mascarpone and folding in the mussels and spice mix.

Because these macarons become soft very quickly after adding the filling, serve them straight after filling them! Pipe a swirl of filling on one biscuit and put a second one on top. You can also serve the filling separate in a bowl. This way, the macarons can be eaten as savoury 'toast'.

appetizer macarons